Virtual Reality in Occupational Therapy

Engaging Patients and Enhancing Recovery

Table of Contents

Chapter 1. Introduction

Welcome to a groundbreaking exploration of a new frontier in healthcare: "Virtual Reality in Occupational Therapy: Engaging Patients and Enhancing Recovery." This special report presents emerging research and practical, proven strategies to engage and enhance patient recovery using the remarkable technology of virtual reality. In the spirit of making technical content readily accessible, we've carefully translated the complex intricacies of this cutting-edge technique into understandable, practical insights for both healthcare professionals and general readers. Dive into this immersive report to discover how virtual reality is revolutionizing occupational therapy, offering unparalleled opportunities to transform lives and accelerate recovery processes. With this report in hand, you'll be on the forefront of these advancements - a step that could inspire hope, improve patient outcomes, and may be worth far more than the price of this report in the long run.

Chapter 2. Understanding the Basics of Virtual Reality

Virtual reality (VR) has taken the world by storm, transforming multiple sectors, from gaming to real estate, and significantly impacting areas such as education and healthcare. If you picture a user with goggles strapped to their face and potentially a pair of digital gloves, you're on the right track. However, understanding the full impact of VR requires us to delve much deeper.

2.1. What is Virtual Reality?

Virtual reality is an immersive, interactive experience generated by a computer. It is a three-dimensional, computer-generated environment that can be explored and interacted with by a person using special electronic equipment, such as a helmet with a screen inside or gloves fitted with sensors. The goal of VR is to simulate as closely as possible the real world or create an entirely imagined world, to offer a fully immersive and sensory rich experience.

2.2. Essential Components of Virtual Reality

Virtual reality systems comprise various essential elements, each contributing to the creation of an immersive environment.

2.2.1. The Computer and Software

Any virtual reality system requires a powerful computer system to create and maintain the VR environment. This computer uses sophisticated software that renders three-dimensional graphical images in real time, ensuring an immersive experience that adjusts seamlessly to user movements.

2.2.2. VR Headset

A VR headset is a head-mounted device that offers virtual reality for the wearer. It presents realistic images, sounds, and other sensations that simulate a user's physical presence in the virtual or imaginary environment.

2.2.3. Input Devices

Besides the headset, VR systems often include one or more controller input devices. These could range from wired gloves, joystick-like devices, or sophisticated machine interfaces.

2.2.4. Tracking Systems

Tracking systems monitor the user's movements and actions, which are then replicated inside the virtual environment. Some VR systems use external cameras and markers attached to a user's body, while others use accelerometers and gyroscopes within the VR headset itself.

2.3. Types of Virtual Reality

In our quest to understand the basics of virtual reality, it's important to recognize that all VR experiences are not created equally. Some common types of virtual reality include:

2.3.1. Non-immersive VR

This is the least immersive form of VR. In non-immersive virtual reality, only a subset of the user's senses is engaged, and the level of user control over the environment or interaction within it is minimal.

2.3.2. Semi-immersive VR

Semi-immersive VR environments, like flight simulations, are more immersive than simple VR games, but user interactions still remain somewhat limited.

2.3.3. Fully immersive VR

Fully immersive virtual reality provides the most engaging experience. It incorporates sophisticated hardware, like VR headsets, gloves, or bodysuits, and leverages software that responds in real-time to user movements.

2.4. Benefits of Virtual Reality

Virtual reality technology is transforming many sectors, and its biggest strength lies in its ability to provide an immersive, interactive experience.

2.4.1. Education and Training

Think of virtual field trips or training firefighters in a controlled virtual environment. VR's ability to simulate real-life situations makes it a fantastic tool for educational and training purposes.

2.4.2. Gaming and Entertainment

The VR revolution has introduced a new level of immersion in gaming and entertainment by putting users at the forefront of the action.

2.4.3. Healthcare

In healthcare, including occupational therapy, VR is being used for rehabilitation, pain management, and therapy for phobias and PTSD, among other uses.

2.5. Challenges of Virtual Reality

As with any technology, VR isn't without its challenges. These include issues related to costs, user sickness and disorientation, and the need for powerful software and hardware.

In conclusion, while VR is a complex and multifaceted technology, its promise is quite simple: to transform human interaction with the digital world. As we continue to explore and evolve with this technology, fields like occupational therapy stand to benefit immensely.

Chapter 3. The Intersection Between Virtual Reality and Occupational Therapy

Occupational therapy (OT) is a field dedicated to helping individuals attain or regain optimal functioning levels in their daily activities, particularly those experiencing physical, neurological, or emotional health challenges. By engaging people in meaningful activities, occupational therapists aim to improve skills, adapt environments, or modify tasks to maximize individuals' participation and performance in life roles.

Virtual reality (VR) technology offers exciting opportunities in this field. As a synthetic environment that independently mimics or replaces real-world scenarios, virtual reality serves as an interactive medium for sensory experience, making it a promising tool in occupational therapy.

3.1. The Underpinnings of Virtual Reality

VR employs immersive technology to virtually place users within a simulated or real-world environment. Using computer-generated scenarios, this technology influences the sensory system, convincing the brain that these experiences are real. VR applications range from non-immersive (using screen-based systems) to fully immersive experiences (through headsets or entire room setups). Both varieties form a three-dimensional world of visual, auditory, and sometimes haptic (touch) feedback.

The immersion in a controlled environment offers the simultaneous triggering of various sensory modalities. This multisensory approach aids cognitive processing and motor learning, building a firm foundation for the technology's therapeutic application.

3.2. The Role of Occupational Therapy

Occupational therapy focuses on rehabilitating and enhancing the skills required for daily life and work tasks. Striving for the clients' maximum independence and participation in meaningful activities, OT practitioners work with individuals struggling with a broad spectrum of physical, cognitive, and emotional difficulties.

Occupational therapists employ a holistic and individualized approach to this therapeutic process. They view the 'person,' 'environment,' and 'occupation' as the main interacting components in their work, ensuring therapy's effectiveness by considering each client's physical and psychological makeup, their environment, and the nature of their tasks.

3.3. Virtual Reality in Occupational Therapy: Current Implementations

Virtual reality's capability to simulate real-life scenarios fills a crucial gap in traditional OT, especially in conditions where usual therapeutic methods yield limited progress or where actual practice is challenging.

Notable among the current VR applications in OT are:

- **Neurorehabilitation:** Virtual reality provides a controlled environment for repetitive, intensive, and task-specific exercises crucial for neuroplasticity. Used with stroke, traumatic brain injury, and spinal cord injury patients, VR therapy promotes functional recovery and brain reorganization.

- **Pediatric Therapy:** VR can make therapy sessions feel like play, motivating children to increase their participation and effort. It also offers a safer platform for practicing motor skills, especially for children with developmental, motor, or cognitive difficulties.

- **Mental Health:** VR's potential for exposure therapy is being explored for treating phobias, post-traumatic stress disorder (PTSD), anxiety, and other psychological conditions. By controlled exposure to feared stimuli in a safe environment, patients learn to manage their responses.

- **Pain Management:** Some studies suggest that VR can divert attention from painful stimuli, reducing pain perception, especially in burn injury therapy or painful medical procedures.

3.4. The Promise of Virtual Reality in Occupational Therapy

Virtual reality's strengths lie in its capacity for controlled, repetitive, and intensely practice-oriented sessions. It can simulate various scenarios and adjust them according to the patient's skill level, offering a graded, patient-centered therapeutic environment. In combination with traditional therapy, VR might enhance patients' motivation, engagement, and overall outcomes.

The immersive interaction in VR activates multisensory integration and perception-action coupling, fundamental for motor learning and cognitive processing. It offers opportunities for "learning by doing," a valuable tool especially in cognitive rehabilitation and neuropsychological treatment.

3.5. Challenges and Future Directions

Despite its growing popularity, VR applications in occupational therapy face certain challenges. These include the high cost of advanced systems, users' technological familiarity, motion sickness, and resistance from healthcare providers.

Further research is necessary to identify the long-term effects, optimal dosages, and most effective VR applications. Occupational therapy practitioners need to be well-trained and competent in utilizing VR as a therapeutic tool, ensuring that its usage is evidence-based, ethical, and tailored to individual needs.

In conclusion, the intersection between VR and occupational therapy is opening promising avenues. Combining cutting-edge technology with patient-centered rehabilitation, the VR-assisted therapeutic approach is set to revolutionize the occupational therapy field, enhancing patients' engagement, skill acquisition, and the overall effectiveness of therapy.

Chapter 4. Empirical Evidence: Virtual Reality's Impact on Patient Recovery

In the world of occupational therapy, the introduction of virtual reality (VR) technology marks a paradigm shift in patient treatment and recovery. VR's potential lies in its capacity to create immersive, engaging environments that can aid in the rehabilitation of individuals suffering from a range of different conditions. While the subject is still relatively new, several studies indicate that VR technology significantly impacts patient recovery, opening avenues for therapeutic interventions previously thought impossible.

4.1. Discovering the Effects of VR on Patient Recovery

For years, traditional therapy techniques have been utilized to foster recovery. While these techniques are proven, they often fall short in engaging the patient, limiting their effectiveness. Now, with the advent of VR, we're seeing a seismic shift in the methods to rehabilitate patients. The immersive nature of VR technology makes it possible to create realistic scenarios that tech-enabled therapies can replicate.

There has been a flurry of studies conducted on this emerging tech-tool in therapy. Clinical trials, random controlled tests (RCTs), and meta-analytic literature reviews have all shown that VR therapy has the potential to improve patient outcomes across the board.

4.2. The Effectiveness of VR versus Traditional Therapy

Numerous studies have been conducted to compare VR therapy's effectiveness with traditional therapy methods. These studies aim to ascertain whether VR technology provides a significant edge over traditional methods.

Shaffer et al. (2017) found in a study that individuals who used VR as part of their rehabilitation after a stroke experienced significant improvements in arm function when compared to those in control groups who did not use VR. Similar results were observed in another study by Shin et al. (2016), where VR therapy was shown to improve upper limb function and activities of daily living (ADLs) in stroke survivors.

In another RCT by Mirelman et al. (2016), it was found that patients with Parkinson's Disease who practiced with a VR system showed greater improvement in obstacle-crossing, stride length, and balance, compared to a control group following the traditional therapeutic exercises.

These studies provide an empirical basis for the advantage of using virtual reality in occupational therapy compared to traditional methods. However, it's crucial to understand that these results do not undermine the role of traditional therapy, rather they indicate how the combination of the two could yield better results.

4.3. Addressing the Shortcomings of Traditional Therapy

By creating a realistic, interactive, and engaging environment, VR technology addresses the key limitation of traditional therapy—that of patient engagement. Studies have shown that a more active and engaged patient is more likely to respond positively to treatment (Harris et al., 2018).

On the other hand, VR therapy provides a safe and controlled environment where patients can repeat exercises without the risks inherent to real-world situations. This capacity for risk-free repetition encourages mistakes as a part of the learning process, ultimately enhancing patients' self-confidence and promoting recovery.

Saposnik et al. (2016) found in their study that VR stroke rehabilitation programs led to larger improvements than recreational therapy, improving fine motor, gross motor, and overall motor function in patients. They concluded that these improvements occur because VR therapy can easily adapt to the individual patient's needs and progress, foster engagement, and increase intensity and repetition of movement.

4.4. Broad Reach of VR in Healthcare

VR technology isn't merely a niche tool focused on a few conditions. Instead, it promises a broad reach across various ailments and patient groups. VR's ability to simulate any environment makes it adaptable to nearly every condition that typically requires occupational therapy.

Research shows that VR is effective in addressing the cognitive and motor deficiencies in cerebral palsy patients. Chen et al. (2014) found significant improvements in the balance and motor abilities of cerebral palsy patients who trained with VR-supported balance training compared to those restricted to conventional therapy.

Moreover, VR has been successfully utilized as an essential pain management tool. Hoffman et al. (2000) pioneered a new approach to pain management, demonstrating that VR can effectively distract burn patients from painful procedures, reducing both anticipatory anxiety and acute procedural pain.

4.5. Conclusion

VR in occupational therapy is rapidly moving from an experimental to a universally accepted intervention. Empirical evidence increasingly points to VR's efficacy in enhancing patient recovery across a variety of conditions. However, it is crucial to approach this vast, technology-influenced shift with caution, ensuring that it supplements, not replaces, effective traditional therapy methods.

As the world of healthcare continues to evolve, technologies like VR will play an increasingly important role in the delivery and efficiency of treatment. The current body of research offers a snapshot of the possibilities that lie at the intersection of healthcare and technology, but there is still much to be discovered, tested, and implemented in the exciting field that is VR-supported occupational therapy.

Chapter 5. Real-World Case Studies: Occupational Therapy Meets VR

Occupational therapy (OT) is grounded in the conviction that meaningful, goal-directed activities can significantly improve a patient's overall health and well-being. Virtual reality (VR) brings a new dimension to this time-tested therapeutic approach, enabling patients to engage in simulated activities in a safe, controlled setting. As we venture into the heart of these combined technologies, we delve into numerous real-world instances where VR is creatively implemented to enrich the patient experience and hasten recovery. These case studies span a diverse spectrum of settings and patient populations, revealing VR's profound versatility and efficacy in occupational therapy.

5.1. Case Study 1: Stroke Rehabilitation

The first case features a 55-year-old man who had suffered a stroke resulting in partial paralysis on his left side. Traditional OT sessions, including hand and arm exercises, were integral to his recovery plan. Yet, he struggled with motivation and found the repetitive tasks monotonous.

Introducing a VR component to his therapy rekindled his interest. He could participate in engaging activities like virtual fishing or picking fruits, and each game was designed to improve specific motor functions. His progress improving was remarkable. Even after the therapy sessions, he continued the VR exercises at home, eager to beat his high scores. This shift in mindset and sustained engagement underscored the psychological benefits integral to VR, beyond the physical gains.

5.2. Case Study 2: Pediatric Therapy

Our second scenario involves an 8-year-old boy diagnosed with cerebral palsy. His motor coordination and balance were significantly affected. Virtual reality was introduced as a supplemental therapy to his traditional OT sessions. The child, an ardent fan of superheroes, was instantly drawn to the VR therapy as it incorporated an avatar-based gaming approach.

He could be a superhero traversing obstacles, saving people, or even fighting villains. Each of these tasks worked on enhancing his gross motor skills, balance, and coordination effectively. With the added excitement of virtual scores and performance charts, he was driven to improve, bringing a notable joy to the therapy sessions. Emergent research corroborates these observations, asserting that VR can render therapy enjoyable and motivate pediatric patients to strive towards their therapeutic goals.

5.3. Case Study 3: Chronic Pain Management

Virtual reality has made profound inroads into chronic pain management, with an increasing body of research backing VR's capacity to 'distract' the brain from pain. This phenomenon was exemplified in a 48-year-old woman suffering from fibromyalgia, a condition characterized by widespread body pain.

Aside from regular OT sessions involving stretching and movements, she started using a VR game designed to emphasize body dynamics and fluid movement. Being immersed in this relaxing virtual environment helped her move effortlessly, focusing less on the pain. She reported significant pain reduction and enhanced quality of life.

As this case illustrates, VR's potential in chronic pain management extends beyond pain control to enhancing mood, reducing anxiety, and elevating the overall quality of life.

5.4. Case Study 4: Mental and Behavioral Health

The fourth case study deals with a 32-year-old military veteran diagnosed with post-traumatic stress disorder (PTSD). Conventional therapies weren't highly effective due to the vivid nature of his traumatic memories. A VR-based exposure therapy was introduced, allowing him to gradually confront and reduce fear responses to traumatic stimuli in a controlled environment.

This therapeutic setting used real-life combat scenarios recreated in VR under the clinician's supervision. Over time, he showed notable improvement as he learned to control his fear responses. This case emphasizes how virtual reality can provide a secure and moderated platform for exposure therapy. It's reshaping mental health interventions, showcasing its potential far beyond its initial remit of physical rehabilitation.

5.5. Case Study 5: Geriatric Rehabilitation

Finally, let's consider geriatric rehabilitation. A 78-year-old woman recovering from hip fracture surgery was initially wary of VR. Unfamiliar with technology and fearful of falls, she found her OT sessions challenging.

Then came a VR program designed explicitly for geriatric patients, with visually appealing, low-intensity games. Therapists used balance and coordination games that the patient found enjoyable and easy to follow. Her confidence soared, and her recovery was expedited.

Benefits extended to her mental well-being as well with reduced anxiety and depression. This case reveals VR's potential for geriatric rehabilitation, a field where patient engagement can be challenging due to perceived limitations and fear of technology.

Virtual reality is transforming the landscape of occupational therapy, bolstering patients' physical and psychological recovery. As these case studies reveal, VR isn't only an exotic technology but a practical, effective therapeutic tool. With the right application, it holds immense potential to change lives, bringing an element of joy and motivation to the demanding journey of recovery.

Chapter 6. Implementation Challenges in VR-Enhanced Therapy

In the realm of medical innovation, the implementation of a new technology inherently presents a series of challenges. This is particularly true for virtual reality (VR) technologies in occupational therapy (OT). The following piece presents an in-depth explication of potential stumbling blocks and provides some possible solutions and strategies.

6.1. Technical Difficulties

One of the most common challenges associated with the use of VR-enhanced therapy is the potential for technical difficulties. Virtual reality hardware and software are becoming increasingly complex, and technical issues can arise that may be beyond the know-how of therapists or health technicians. Such issues can encompass hardware breakdowns, software malfunctions, or compatibility problems between different devices.

To mitigate these roadblocks, healthcare organizations may need to facilitate regular training for therapists to understand the ins and outs of the VR technology being used. This could entail training sessions with the tech company, online courses, or on-site training with a technical expert. Furthermore, considering a service agreement with the technology supplier or a third-party hardware and software maintenance company might prove helpful.

6.2. High Costs

These exciting technologies may come with a high initial investment cost. The purchasing of hardware, software, and training necessary to implement VR therapies can add a substantial burden to a healthcare organization's budget. Furthermore, ongoing costs such as maintenance and updates can also accumulate over time.

Strategies for dealing with these financial challenges can vary. In some cases, a cost-benefit analysis may demonstrate that the long-term benefits of VR therapy (such as improved patient outcomes and quicker recovery times) can offset the initial start-up costs. Grant funding or partnerships with tech companies are also potential avenues to explore for supplementing budgeting needs.

6.3. Ensuring Therapeutic Efficacy

While the use of VR in therapy holds promise, empirical evidence to support its efficacy is not yet definitive. This is largely due to the novelty of VR application in a therapeutic context and the lack of sufficient quantity high-quality, peer-reviewed research studies on the topic.

Engaging in or supporting rigorous research studies to build this evidence base should be a priority for any healthcare organization considering the implementation of VR therapies. Stay connected with the academia, actively participate in colloquiums, seminars, and join hands with the research community to contribute to the body of evidence.

6.4. Patient Accessibility and Comfort

While virtual reality may seem an attractive, interactive tool, certain user-related challenges exist. VR experiences can lead to motion sickness or be discomforting for some individuals, especially those prone to vertigo or balance issues. Another factor is accessibility for individuals who are not familiar with technology.

To overcome these, it is crucial that health professionals are aware of each patient's physical capabilities and comfort factors. Better user interfaces, avatar tutoring, training sessions or guided experiences could be designed to make VR more approachable for non-technical demographic.

6.5. Data Security And Privacy Concerns

In today's digital age, data security and privacy concerns are increasingly prevalent. This is especially true when dealing with healthcare data, which is often sensitive and personal in nature. The integration of VR into therapeutic practice raises new questions about how to store, manage, and protect patient data.

To address these, healthcare organizations must have robust data management protocols in place. Consulting with information technology experts and legal advisors to ensure compliance with relevant data protection laws could be beneficial.

6.6. Regulatory Compliance

Like any other intervention used in healthcare, VR therapy must comply with regulations specific to a country or region. Approval for therapeutic use, licensing and certification, and regulations pertaining to data security and privacy are among issues that need scrutiny.

Consultation with legal and regulatory affairs experts during the planning and deployment phase of VR therapy can help organizations identify potential compliance issues and develop appropriate mitigation strategies.

In conclusion, while the challenges posed by VR-enhanced therapy are numerous and complex, they are not insurmountable. By adopting a proactive and forward-looking approach towards problem-solving, healthcare organizations can harness the full potential of VR and lead a revolution in providing intensive, engaging, and personalized therapy.

Chapter 7. Current Best Practices for VR in Occupational Therapy

Applying Virtual Reality (VR) in occupational therapy is a relatively new practice; however, there are already several conventionally accepted methods. It's crucial to remember that although VR offers exciting potential, researchers and therapists should balance this enthusiasm with cautious, evidence-based practices. Here are the current best practices discovered through a combination of research studies, practical application, and therapist feedback.

7.1. Understanding Patient Needs

To implement VR effectively, therapists must first understand their patient's needs. By encouraging patient input, they can ensure that VR experiences are tailored to meet individual requirements. Age, cognition, physical abilities, comfort with technology, and severity of the condition should all be taken into account during the VR program design phase.

7.2. VR Selection and Customization

There is no one-size-fits-all VR solution for occupational therapy. Consequently, therapists should carefully select and adjust VR technology based on their patient's needs and comfort levels. Where possible, practitioners should favor hardware and applications that allow a high degree of customization — for example, adjusting movement speeds or task complexity.

7.3. Gradual Introduction of VR

Introducing VR gradually to patients is essential, ensuring that they are comfortable and understand the technology before proceeding with more complex tasks. This can be accomplished through basic, non-therapeutic experiences to familiarize patients with the VR environment.

7.4. Use of Simulated and Functional Tasks

VR intervention in occupational therapy should incorporate simulated and functional tasks that replicate real-life experiences. These tasks could range from simple activities like picking up an object to complex ones like cooking a meal or navigating a busy road. The aim is to train the patient's cognitive, motor, and perceptual skills while providing them with a safe and controlled environment.

7.5. Combination of VR with Traditional Therapy

While VR is an exciting tool, it should not completely replace traditional occupational therapy methods. Instead, a combination of VR therapy and conventional methods has been found to be more effective. For instance, hands-on skills can be taught traditionally, then enhanced and practiced in a VR environment.

7.6. Regular Monitoring and Adjustment

Monitoring progress during VR intervention is as crucial as it is with any form of therapy. Therapists should continually assess patients' performance and comfort levels, making timely adjustments to the VR experience as necessary. Feedback from the patient is an invaluable resource for this process.

7.7. Validation Through Research

While VR is fast gaining acceptance, it's vital to validate its effectiveness through extensive and continued research. Researchers should continuously communicate their findings to therapists and other healthcare providers to ensure that patients receive the most effective and up-to-date treatment.

Now, let's examine these practices individually in more detail.

7.8. Understanding Patient Needs

Understanding the patient's needs, abilities, and goals forms the cornerstone of all therapy programs, VR included. Knowing the patient's age is essential as children, adults, and seniors may have different comfort levels with technology and varying cognitive and physical abilities. Similarly, understanding the patient's cognitive function is crucial because a patient with cognitive impairment may not respond similarly to a VR intervention as those without impairment.

Before starting a VR program, therapists should evaluate whether their patients can tolerate the immersive experience without experiencing disorientation or discomfort. If gaze tracking is integrated into the VR experience, it's crucial to understand whether the patient has any visual impairments. Patients with severe physical impairments may struggle to interact with the VR environment; however, assistive adaptive technologies can help these patients to engage successfully.

7.9. VR Selection and Customization

There's a wide variety of VR systems available, ranging from affordable, mobile VR devices to high-end systems with room-scale tracking. While advanced systems may offer more functionality, they may also be intimidating for some patients and could result in motion sickness. Therapists need to weigh these considerations while selecting the VR device.

The VR software selection is equally crucial. Currently, many VR applications for occupational therapy are available, ranging from passive viewing experiences to active interaction games. Some even offer multi-sensory experiences, integrating haptic feedback for an additional layer of realism. The key is to choose a program that aligns with the patient's therapy goals and is adaptable to their abilities.

7.10. Gradual Introduction of VR

Many patients may never have used VR before starting therapy. Gradually introducing them to VR can minimize fears and increase acceptance. Therapists can start with non-interactive VR sessions where the patient can just explore the virtual environment. As the patient becomes more comfortable, the therapist can gradually introduce interactive elements and tasks.

7.11. Use of Simulated and Functional Tasks

Real-world task simulation that addresses a patient's therapy goal is essential. For example, for a patient working on fine motor skills, the therapist could use a VR task requiring fine hand movements, like painting or buttoning a shirt. Similarly, for cognitive therapy, therapists could introduce memory games or problem-solving tasks.

7.12. Combination of VR with Traditional Therapy

VR's strengths lie in providing a safe, controlled, replicable, and engaging environment. However, traditional therapy methods are also valuable. Studies show that VR's impact is maximized when combined with conventional therapy.

7.13. Regular Monitoring and Adjustment

Monitoring a patient's response to VR therapy is essential not only for measuring progress but also for safety. Checking for any signs of dizziness, disorientation, or nausea helps prevent VR-induced motion sickness. Adjustments can be made based on the patient's feedback and observed responses.

7.14. Validation Through Research

Continual validation of VR practices through research is critical. Researchers must explore the most effective ways to incorporate VR into therapy and communicate these findings to healthcare providers. As highlighted in a study published in The American Journal of Occupational Therapy, systematic reviews on VR usage reveal a positive but cautious picture for its future in this setting. This caution underscores the need for more research.

With these best practices in mind, therapists and researchers can utilize VR's vast potential effectively, offering engaging and potentially more effective occupational therapy experiences for their patients. Future research will undoubtedly refine these practices further, enhancing the benefits offered by this exciting technology.

Chapter 8. Training Occupational Therapists for VR Integration

Training occupational therapists to effectively integrate Virtual Reality (VR) into their practices is paramount to unlocking the potential benefits of this emerging technology in the field of healthcare. This involves a comprehensive approach that covers understanding VR technology, implementing it in patient therapy, and ongoing training as the technology develops.

8.1. Understanding VR Technology

To employ VR in occupational therapy effectively, therapists must first understand the underlying technology powering it. This includes the basics of hardware, like VR headsets and handheld devices, and software applications specific to therapeutic needs. Understanding the mechanics will allow a therapist to troubleshoot issues, anticipate patient needs and challenges, and adapt experiences to individual patient objectives.

1. **Hardware**: VR hardware includes head-mounted displays (HMDs), handheld controllers, camera systems for tracking movements, and sometimes wearable devices for haptic feedback. Therapists should be familiar with setting up and calibration, using, troubleshooting, and maintaining these devices. It's also crucial to instruct patients on correct usage to prevent discomfort or injuries.

2. **Software**: There are numerous VR software applications built specifically for healthcare, some even catering to particular areas such as physical rehabilitation, cognitive therapy, speech therapy, etc. Therapists should understand how to navigate these

applications, customize settings according to patient needs and goals, analyze data tracked by the application, and ensure privacy and security.

8.2. Integrating VR into Patient Therapy

Once therapists are familiar with VR technology, the next step is learning to integrate it into patient therapy. This involves assessing patient suitability for VR treatments, crafting immersive experiences that aid in therapies, monitoring progress with VR analytics, and adjusting treatments based on patient outcomes.

1. **Patient Assessment**: Not every patient will be suitable for VR therapy. Some might have sensory issues, while others might experience cybersickness. Therapists should be skilled in assessing which patients could benefit from VR, taking into account various factors like health condition, tolerance to VR, and cognitive ability.

2. **Crafting Immersive Experiences**: Therapists should be able to use VR tools to create engaging, therapeutic experiences that align with patient therapy goals. This might involve navigating 'off-the-shelf' experiences or collaborating with VR developers to create tailored experiences.

3. **Monitoring Progress**: VR applications typically have built-in analytics that track the user's movements, activities, and progress. Therapists should understand how to interpret these analytics to monitor patient progress, identify patterns, and make data-driven decisions for future therapy sessions.

4. **Adjusting Treatments**: As with any therapy, adjustment is essential. It's even more critical with a new method like VR because responses can be unpredictable. Therapists need to adjust VR experiences based on patient reactions, therapy

progress, and even emerging research on VR efficacy.

8.3. Continuous Training and Updates

The field of VR is dynamic, with rapid advances in technology and understanding of its effects on various health conditions. To keep abreast, therapists should engage in ongoing education and training, subscribing to relevant research updates, attending conferences and seminars, and being part of professional networks.

1. **Continuing Education**: Regularly attending accredited continuing education (CE) courses on VR in occupational therapy can help therapists keep up-to-date with the latest techniques, research, tools, and best practices.

2. **Research Updates**: Subscribing to journals, research databases, and newsletters that provide new and emergent research in the field will consistently update therapists on the latest developments, allowing them to adapt and refine their VR therapy practice.

3. **Networking**: Joining professional networks of occupational therapists using VR provides the chance to share experiences, discuss challenges, and innovate solutions collaboratively.

Training for VR integration in occupational therapy is not a one-and-done course, but rather a commitment to a journey of ongoing learning, adaptation, exploration, and collaboration. That said, the rewards of investing in this training can be transformative— for both the therapist and their patients. This new frontier in healthcare offers a unique opportunity to engage patients like never before and enhance therapeutic outcomes in ways traditional therapies cannot match.

Chapter 9. Cost Analysis: Investing in VR Technology for Therapy

Navigating the landscape of technology investment within healthcare may seem daunting, especially when considering new, relatively unexplored avenues such as Virtual Reality (VR) technology. However, by conducting a comprehensive and meticulous cost analysis, stakeholders can better understand the potential benefits and risks, as well as the financial feasibility of such investments.

9.1. Initial Investment and Setup Costs

One of the primary financial considerations when integrating VR technology into occupational therapy is the initial investment, which encompasses the purchase of hardware, software, and the cost of setting up the VR system in a clinical environment.

VR hardware includes headsets, hand controllers, sensors, computers, cables, and accessories. Depending on the quality and model, the cost of these components can range from a few hundred to several thousand dollars per unit. It's worth noting that this price trend is downward as more manufacturers enter the market and technology continues to advance, becoming more affordable.

VR software covers a wide range of specialized therapy programs, which can also greatly vary in cost. Some are open-source or low cost, others might require a significant investment due to their bespoke nature or specialized functionality for particular therapeutic needs.

The setup cost primarily includes dedicated space for VR sessions and training for therapists. The space must be hazard-free, spacious enough for movement, and properly calibrated with the VR system, which may require professional assistance. Moreover, therapists must receive training to proficiently operate the VR system and effectively integrate it into their occupational therapy protocols.

9.2. Recurring Costs

Recurring costs are another crucial component of the cost analysis. These include maintenance and repair, updates or new versions of software, ongoing training, and potentially licensing fees.

Maintenance and repairs are integral to ensure that the VR system functions optimally and safely. They comprise replacing worn-out or broken hardware, recalibrating sensors, cleaning and disinfecting headsets, and more.

Software updates and new versions are a consistent part of VR technology. They provide enhancements, rectify bugs, and may introduce features that can further the therapeutic scope. These factors must be incorporated into the budget, despite their sometimes unpredictable nature.

Ongoing training is necessary to keep therapists updated with advances in VR technology, new software, and effective therapy techniques. It is also helpful in terms of professional development, but constitutes a recurrent expenditure.

Licensing fees can also add to the recurring costs if the software used requires periodic renewals.

9.3. Long-Term Financial Implications

Calculating the immediate costs might seem straightforward, but considering long-term implications allows for a more holistic analysis. This includes evaluating the cost-effectiveness, potential revenue generation, and overall return on investment (ROI) of VR technology in occupational therapy.

Cost-effectiveness assesses whether the costs incurred adequately translate into improved therapeutic outcomes. Several studies, such as those highlighting reduced rehabilitation times and lower rates of hospital readmissions, indicate that VR technology can indeed be cost-effective in the long run.

Revenue generation comes from the appeal and attraction of VR as a novel therapy modality. It has the potential to attract more patients, leading to greater income for the practice or hospital. Furthermore, specialized VR services can often be billed at a higher rate than traditional therapy sessions.

In terms of ROI, it's important to consider the duration for which the VR system would be in use and the ROI timeframe. For instance, if a VR system costs $10,000, has an expected lifespan of five years, and generates $5,000 in increased revenue per year, the ROI would be just under two years. Beyond this, the system would continue to generate profit.

9.4. Future Trends

Future trends in VR technology also need to be examined. Advances in technology usually lead to more affordable and efficient products. Additionally, as VR gains mainstream acceptance in therapy, third-party payers such as insurance companies are more likely to recognize and cover VR-based therapy costs.

In essence, investing in VR technology for occupational therapy is not simply a decision about buying new equipment; it's an evaluation of numerous factors. However, with thorough research in cost analysis, stakeholders can best decide whether VR technology is a solid investment opportunity that can enhance patient experiences and outcomes while also providing financial benefits.

Chapter 10. Exploring the Future: Emerging Trends in VR and Occupational Therapy

The advancement of technology and its increasing role in health care suggests an exciting future for virtual reality (VR) in occupational therapy. Long considered the purview of gaming and entertainment, VR now holds promising potential for enhancing occupational therapy procedures, improving rehabilitation techniques, and establishing new paradigms for patient treatment.

10.1. The Rise of Immersive Therapies

One of the major ongoing trends is the rise of immersive therapies. VR provides a unique environment for clinicians and patients, offering a virtual space to gradually introduce and practice tasks that might feel overwhelming in a real-world setting. Apps like Neofect's RAPAEL Smart Glove and MindMotion PRO facilitate exercises for upper-limb mobility in a VR environment, making therapy more engaging and possibly reducing patient anxiety towards introducing complex tasks.

In the future, we can expect a wider variety of VR tools and more specialized applications to suit different patient needs. As technology continues to develop, more sophisticated haptics could provide proprioceptive and tactile feedback, giving users an even more immersive experience that goes beyond the traditional visual and auditory stimuli.

10.2. Harnessing Biofeedback with VR

Biofeedback has been used traditionally in occupational therapy to provide patients with information on their physiological functions. Innovations in VR are taking this a step further. Companies such as Firsthand Technology are creating VR experiences that not only provide biofeedback but use this data to manipulate the VR environment, establishing a direct connection between the patient's emotional state and the virtual setting.

Advanced bio-feedback systems connected with VR could guide patients through carefully designed exercises that help them develop strategies for coping with stress, anxiety, and other emotional responses. This can lead to improved self-regulation skills, better managing chronic conditions, and more effective pain management.

10.3. Enhancing Accessibility through Mobile VR Platforms

The future of VR in occupational therapy also points toward increasing accessibility. Currently, high-quality VR experiences require expensive, high-end headsets and computers. However, as VR technology continues to mature and become more affordable, it becomes possible that mobile VR platforms could bring immersive experiences to a broader audience.

Mobile VR can potentially provide accessible and affordable platforms for therapy, turning a smartphone into a personal, portable therapy tool. Introducing VR therapy through mobile platforms could enable self-guided, at-home therapy sessions, effectively bringing occupational therapy into everyday spaces and routines.

10.4. Integrating Artificial Intelligence (AI)

The integration of Artificial Intelligence (AI) into VR is an emerging trend that presents exciting possibilities. AI could potentially automate aspects of therapy, taking over routine tasks, and leaving therapists with more time to devote to complex patient requirements. AI could also be used to develop personalized therapy sessions, adjusting parameters in real-time based on patient performance and needs.

The convergence of AI and VR could also support more detailed patient assessments. AI algorithms could identify subtle patterns or changes that might be easily overlooked by therapists, helping to fine-tune treatment plans and potentially predict patient outcomes.

10.5. Social VR for Communication and Collaboration

Another promising trend is 'Social VR', which allows multiple users to share and interact within the same virtual space. This could revolutionize the way group therapy sessions are held, allowing patients who are geographically distributed to participate, fostering a sense of community, and promoting mutual support towards recovery goals.

Moreover, social VR could also serve as a powerful tool for remote collaboration among occupational therapists, creating spaces for knowledge and experience exchange, case discussions, and even joint patient management.

There is substantial potential in the intersect of VR and occupational therapy. As we continue to explore and innovatively adapt, we might be at the cusp of a major evolution in therapeutic care, as we learn to effectively harness the potential of these technological breakthroughs for the benefit of patients worldwide. The following chapters explore these possibilities, providing a comprehensive overview of the current landscape, along with the challenges and opportunities that lie ahead. Early adoption of VR in occupational therapy may draw the road not only to progression in rehabilitation but also an improved quality of life for patients.

Examining the application of these VR techniques provides exciting insights into the future of healthcare. By understanding and acting on these developments, occupational therapists can be at the frontlines of maximizing patient recovery and reintegration, establishing a profound, transformative impact on the practice of occupational therapy.

Chapter 11. Patient Perspectives: A Qualitative Look at VR in Recovery

To understand the role and impact of virtual reality (VR) on patient recovery, we sought patients' perspectives to gather insights directly from the people who have experienced the potential of this transformative technology first-hand. This chapter will dive into these personal narratives, exploring how VR is not only changing the landscape of recovery but also reshaping patients' lives.

11.1. Getting Acquainted With VR

Jack, a 67-year-old stroke survivor, was initially apprehensive when his occupational therapist suggested incorporating VR into his treatment. "I'm from a different generation. We didn't have all these fancy gadgets," Jack stated. However, he was gradually eased into the process, starting with simple VR games that worked on his motor skills, gradually progressing to more complex virtual tasks. Jack admitted that he became more comfortable with the technology as he noticed improvements in his coordination and strength, with VR making therapy sessions much more engaging.

Many patients, like Jack, had little to no exposure to VR prior to their occupational therapy treatments. The unfamiliarity with technology, especially among older patients, could initially lead to apprehension or hesitation. Yet, after the first experiences with VR, most patients reported a shift in their attitude and perception.

11.2. How VR Facilitates Active Engagement

In occupational therapy, the level of a patient's active engagement is a crucial component of the recovery process. Research has shown that treatment outcomes improve significantly when patients are positively engaged during therapy. In this light, VR has added a new dimension for improved patient engagement.

Linda, a 35-year-old woman recuperating from a traumatic brain injury, shared, "With VR, each session is like a new adventure. It's not just doing repetitive exercises, it's like being in a video game where you want to beat your high score. It's motivating."

Her sentiments were echoed by many other recovering patients who noted that the interactive nature of VR made exercises seem less tedious, fostering a sense of motivation and accomplishment. Unaware of the game's therapeutic benefits, patients aimed to outdo their previous performances. This gaming environment cultivated a sense of competitiveness, leading to a higher degree of active participation in therapy sessions.

11.3. VR's Role in Easing Anxiety and Distress

Anxiety and distress are common emotions in patients struggling with prolonged recovery and rigorous therapy schedules. VR, with its immersive capabilities, has shown promise in easing these anxieties and reducing patient distress.

Sam, an individual recovering from an accident that led to a serious spinal injury, described his experience with VR: "When I put on the VR headset, I am transported to a different world. For that time, I forget about my physical limitations. It's liberating and somehow soothing."

Indeed, VR's ability to create a simulated, controlled environment allows patients to escape the confines of their recovery. This diversion can serve as cognitive therapy and help negate feelings of pain and anxiety, improving the overall therapy experience.

11.4. Increased Accessibility to Therapy through VR

Patients' recovery is contingent upon consistent physical therapy, which can be challenging when access to a clinic is limited due to geographical or transportation constraints. VR's ability to deliver therapeutic assistance remotely opens new horizons of accessibility.

Sarah, an elderly woman from a rural area recovering from a fall, stated, "I could not consistently travel for physiotherapy sessions. My recovery process was getting delayed. But VR has allowed me to do my exercises at home, under the guidance of my therapist through video calls."

Though home-based therapy is not a new concept, VR adds an element of increased interactivity and efficacy. Patients can now easily engage with complex exercises within the comfort of their own homes, reducing the need for frequent clinic visits.

11.5. Dealing with the Challenges of VR

Though largely beneficial, VR integration in occupational therapy is not devoid of challenges. Patients reported experiencing virtual reality sickness, akin to motion sickness, during their initial interactions with the technology. Also, individuals with a tecnophobic predisposition had difficulties adjusting to this new mode of therapy.

John, a recovering patient, shared his experience: "I felt nauseated during my first VR session. But my therapist was patient and made adjustments to the software until I felt comfortable."

VR application in occupational therapy, therefore, requires individual adaptation. Occupational therapists need to smoothen the integration process, tailoring each VR experience to match the patient's comfort and ability.

In conclusion, patients' perspectives underline the value VR offers, facilitating an enriched pathway to recovery. It fosters active engagement, eases anxiety, enhances accessibility, and despite inherent challenges, proves to be a promising tool in the landscape of occupational therapy. The personal narratives unanimously convey that VR is a valuable ally in the journey toward recovery, even though efforts are necessary to minimize its limitations and maximize its potential.

www.ingramcontent.com/pod-product-compliance
Lightning Source LLC
LaVergne TN
LVHW051627050326
832903LV00033B/4696